HOME AND DRY

ANONYMOUS MUMMY

To
K, C, S, A, O, M & D
quite simply you all saved my life.

Thank you forever x

Dear...

I've been meaning to write to you for ages. I've really thought about it a lot, but you know what it's like when you're not really sure how to start. When you want to say something, but you're basically a big coward who would rather procrastinate for years to avoid potential upset.

So, I'm just going to chat to you and then you can choose whether you want to listen to me rattling on or not. You never know though, we might have a bit in common you and me.

I am a fully paid up member of the 'Right Royal Fuck up Club'. I'm also thankfully a living breathing, reasonably happy individual. Life can be a bit tough at times but on the whole, I'm pretty much alright. Don't get me wrong, there are plenty of regular dramas and some of them, I'm proud to say, are not even down to me! A few bumps in the road but that's it, pretty much like most people.

I'm under the radar, nothing special, nothing to write home about. I'm average height, average build, average intelligence. I try to be kind, I am famously forgetful, I love a really good laugh, I'm not at all good at cooking and I'm incredibly intolerant.

This is me now. That pretty much was me before.

So that's it; a forty something, unremarkable, 'pass her by in the street' woman.

But six years ago, alcoholism ripped through my life and tore everything I have away from me and the worst part was, I didn't even see it coming!

You see *it's* not choosy where it forms, the ice that develops under your feet and glides you seamlessly from a social drinker into a problem drinker. You don't need to have had an horrendous childhood or an abusive relationship, alcoholism can develop in anyone, rich or poor, celebrity or general public, it just doesn't matter who you are or where you have come from.

Addiction is a great leveller, every alcoholic or addict I've ever met including myself, started out with the thought that they were different, special in some kind of way. The truth is we are all the same, we can identify with a room full of strangers just like us on the other side of the world. We are everywhere, living in mansions and doorways, we share a common bond and we recognise each other's pain.

Alcoholism is a progressive illness of the soul, if you are drinking alcoholically and you continue you will only sink lower, it's as simple as that. For some the decent is quick; for others it can take years. However, the last few months on the slide to the bottom are usually the same for most people; failing health, insanity, loneliness, anger, despair and terror. The outcome is inevitable and will be the same, vomiting blood and losing control of your bodily functions - whether it's in the gutter or a marble bathroom, it makes no difference. Passed out on the floor in a pool of sick and urine we are all equal.

Recovery though, if you are desperate enough to choose it, is varied, colourful, bloody hard work and most of all, worth it.

I'm going to tell you what happened to me and my

family because if any of what I say rings true with you and you find the courage to seek some help before you lose everything you hold dear, (including your own dignity and sanity), then this letter will have been worth writing.

I look at it this way, what happened to me was so catastrophically destructive that if I can give you a small insight, show you how powerful and baffling an alcohol addiction is and where it can take you, then maybe it will encourage you to get help before you reach the depths that I sunk to. I truly hope so. I am not an expert, I have no training, and I certainly don't have a cure. I can, however, absolutely assure you that you are not alone, that you can stop it in its tracks and you can live a long and 'normal' life free of alcohol. You can even still have a brilliant night out and a damn good laugh. There are the most amazing and inspiring people everywhere who will be delighted to help you, they are all around you, all you have to do is open your eyes, shut down your judgements and ask.

If I'm honest I was already addicted to alcohol and

drinking far too much when I first met the man who became my partner, I think I was quite good fun to be with in the beginning, completely oblivious to the living hell that was only a few months ahead of us. You see, I didn't know it, but the countdown had started and I was fast running out of lovely, woozey, fun drinking time.

I had been functioning for years caped in a red wine comfort blanket, living with my children who had been very young when I stopped drinking for fun and started drinking for comfort.

It was tea, bath and bed for them, crash on the sofa with a bottle for me, with no one to notice and no one to criticise. I was in denial and behind the façade, I was in tatters.

So, one morning when my partner gently suggested that he thought I might be drinking too much, I felt stung and utterly mortified. I got cross, I told him that I thought he was exaggerating and generally being boring, controlling and wrong. I was also extremely unnerved.

For ages, without fail I would open a bottle of wine every evening whilst I was cooking dinner, I would hide it from my children, then I would open another one once they'd gone to bed, wake up on the sofa at silly o'clock in the morning, finish any wine that was still in the bottle or open another one and down a glass before eventually climbing into bed.

That was every night!

I would get up in the morning like nothing had happened and get my children to school and myself off to work. I might be a bit shaky, but a few strong coffees and something sugary usually sorted that out. Anyway, I only had to get through the day and then I could get home, get dinner on the go and have a drink, just like everyone else that I knew.

I would justify my drinking to myself by saying that I probably wouldn't drink over the weekend, I would have a bit of a break and it was only all the stress I was under that made me drink through the week, I could take it or leave it at weekends.

It wasn't long before my partner knew differently.

I was regularly staying at his house and he could see that things were not OK. For him, it wasn't just the amount I was drinking that worried him, it was my obsession with it, the careful planning that I put in to making sure that I had a supply. Without fail there was always wine in the house. If by any chance there wasn't, which was rare, I would offer to drive anywhere to get it, at any time of the day or night. I wouldn't take no for an answer and I would make up elaborate reasons for why I needed to go shopping so that I could secretly replenish supplies.

That first large glass of wine every night was more important to me than anything else on the planet.

If for some reason I couldn't drink one night, perhaps because I had to pick my partner or my children up from something, I would be a brat. Angry, short tempered and intolerant, I would throw a huge grown up tantrum until I got what I thought I wanted, whilst having no idea that my body was actually craving.

This went on for a long time, and it wasn't plain sailing, other things were happening. .

If we went out to the pub or to friends' houses, I would insist that my partner drove. If I had to drive, I would struggle to have a good time. I wouldn't be able to relax, chat to people, be amusing and good company. I would literally be counting down the minutes until I could get home and catch up on my drinking, then of course I'd be lovely, but it was too late. I'd have ruined his evening so he would quietly go to bed and leave me to it. Occasionally, he would join me for a couple, but I would get utterly hammered and would usually pass out on the sofa or in bed and not remember any part of the previous evening in the morning.

I always managed to get up in the mornings though, I was still holding down a job and I usually got my children to school on time.

I knew that I wasn't OK, all my friends drank, but none of them drank as much or as quickly as me. On evenings out with them I would make sure I had a good few glasses before I went, then I would find it incredibly frustrating waiting for them to drink up each round before getting the next one in. To make matters worse,

I would usually then upset one of them on the way home. I was losing social skills, I was losing friends and I was fast losing me. I carried on though, every evening the same, keeping most of the balls in the air and avoiding the truth.

It came as a huge shock one evening when I was at my partner's house drinking a large glass of wine at the kitchen table and my close friend turned up out of the blue. Her face was pale and serious, she stood next to my partner united in their concern. I was told that they had been discussing me for a while and were extremely worried about the amount I was drinking.

I was horrified, embarrassed and very ashamed. I was also pretty pissed off. I agreed that I probably drank too much through the week, I would cut it down, maybe only drink moderately at weekends. They were relieved but not convinced, I could see it written on their faces. I did my best to try and persuade them that things were not as bad as they thought and get them to back off. I knew I was drinking too much, but I honestly thought that they were overreacting, I certainly didn't need anybody damn well talking about me behind my back and pointing a finger at me. How dare they? They both drank regularly too – offence became the easiest form of defence. However, I decided that this was the incentive I needed, I would stop drinking and I would damn well show them that they were wrong, sanctimonious bloody hypocrites.

The following night when I tried not to have a drink, I just couldn't do it. I held off for hours, I was hot, shaky and furious, I was also belligerent and worried. I was staying at my partner's house and he was watching me like a hawk, so I came up with a clever plan. I hid a bottle of vodka in the garden, let the dog out a lot and pretended I was sipping diet coke all night. Ha, it worked, I fooled him.

The reality was I didn't fool him, I saddened him to the core, he realised his worst fears were true. I really could not stop. And whilst I was hiding in that cold dark garden with my hidden vodka bottle a little niggle right at the back of mind tore into my thoughts: I was in real trouble. As quickly as I could I drowned the niggly thought in neat vodka straight from the bottle, and it didn't even feel wrong.

I was becoming numb inside and that was what I had wanted for a very long time.

Two

For as long as I can remember I had been unhappy, I was deeply resentful, I was let down, I was disillusioned, I was full of anger about my childhood, my teenage years, my marriage, my choices, bloody everything. Mainly though, and I only know this now, I was overwhelmed with bitterness and anger at myself.

You see for every bad turn that, in my opinion, had been dealt to me, I was there, I didn't have to just take it. I could have stood up for myself, spoken up, protected whatever was important to me at the time, been the brave one, but I didn't. I often apologised for events that were not my doing, turned a blind eye, people-pleased and generally behaved like a willing door mat. The problem with being like that is, it wasn't truly how I felt. I wanted to shout and yell but I had no idea how to appropriately, without blowing things out of proportion or at worst looking like an idiot. Basically, I was full to the brim with debilitating fear and had been my whole life.

I don't just mean, a bit scared. I mean deep rooted, in my blood, my skin, my heart and my head. Fear.

I'm not.................... and I can't...............

Fill in any words you like, they will all be the right ones. I knew it, I didn't just think it, I knew that I was thick, ugly, fat, stupid etc. Don't worry I'm not going to bang on in a 'woe is me' kind of way, I just want to try and get you to see how wrapped up I was in me, what other people thought of me, or, as now I've learnt, what I believed other people thought of me! I've also realised that the me I thought I was, wasn't me at all but a fake me projected into the world to camouflage the fear .

So, I faked everything, people have always told me that I come across as being really confident, that's what I'm talking about. I could convincingly pretend that I was someone else. I would try to emulate women I knew who stood up for themselves, and looked like they were in control, I sort of half managed that for years.

But whilst I was merrily pretending to be someone I'm really not, I was busy squirreling away all the authentic feelings and reactions that I really felt. Anger mainly, into what I thought was the dusty old attic in my head, there to be forgotten and never brought back.

I had plenty of good friends, amazingly most of them are still around now. I worked hard, but I was always acutely aware that I could be knocked off my stride in an instant by a spiky comment or by messing something up, that's when the façade would crumble, and I would be at the mercy of my complete inability to accept failing without falling to pieces. I was like a small child who's done something wrong, one that has been reprimanded, and spends the resulting time either in floods of tears or lashing out at anyone who gets in the way because they don't like how they're feeling and they don't know what to do about it.

On the whole, apart from apologising profusely I managed to keep it all in and stay quiet. I would then indulge in an almighty crisis in my own head which would strengthen my belief that I couldn't do anything right.

The men in my life quickly worked me out, and some of them learned how to deliberately knock me, so that I would drop my fake persona and be all weak and needy. Then of course after a while they'd get fed up with me like that and want to be with someone who didn't behave like a clingy loyal dog, desperate for constant reassurance that they were wanted.

Once on my own again, I'd pick myself up, put on a shiny new fake layer of confidence and off I'd go, another bunch of scars to put in the mental attic. Loads more frustration to live with.

At that time I had a reasonably normal social life and I would not have been considered by anyone as someone who drank too much. In fact, three glasses of wine and I was pissed. It never occurred to me to buy wine in the supermarket as part of the weekly shop. It just wasn't really on my radar.

You see I hadn't learnt how to use alcohol to self-medicate yet. I just treated it as something you had now and again when you went out with your friends. It was only later I realised that it also doubled up very nicely as a magic elixir that could take the sting out of getting through every day. It could make me feel clever, intelligent, very opinionated and more than happy to share those opinions, even to the point of deliberately starting an argument just for the sheer rush of it.

....

I met my future husband in a pub. He was working there, and it was my birthday, ironically the very first thing I ever said to him was. 'Double vodka and diet coke please!' He was impressed, I was flattered. Nobody ever chatted me up, I've always been told that I have 'Fuck off and don't even think about it' etched on my face. I suppose wearing an icy expression was my special mask, designed to protect me. If blokes didn't talk to me, then they couldn't say anything that might hurt me.

My future husband swooped in and swept me off my feet. My last couple of boyfriends had both run off with someone else so I was already pretty broken, my self confidence in shreds. I was just starting to get back up again and desperate for someone to validate me as a remotely attractive person.

He was charming, great fun, intelligent and he thought that I was wonderful, so that was enough for me. The fact that he thought all woman were wonderful didn't seem to ring alarm bells. He made me feel like I was the best, and I absolutely lapped it up.

We ended up living abroad for two years and boy did we drink, but it was never a problem, it never occurred to me to drink at any other time that wasn't a dinner, a lunch, cocktails, whatever. I was just like all the other women that I'd made friends with, Normal!

Looking back, I think the only reason I was drinking normally, was because the rest of my life wasn't real, I didn't look like me, no one knew me, I was enjoying a lovely fake life, with no pressure and no reason to look at the cracks that were forming in my brittle self-confidence and self-worth. My boyfriend was out working everyday so my existence was as important as a chipped ornament, nobody wanted anything from me, I was purely there to have fun, please myself and waste my days. I was perfectly happy with that, I had a lovely time writing, painting and day dreaming about what an amazing future we'd carve out when we got home. When I wasn't doing that the days were spent, sunbathing, shopping, going to the gym and getting ready to go out for dinner and drinks that night. I did a bit of child minding to earn a bit of spending money, but that was the sum total of any pressure that I had to deal with. My life was easy, shallow and spoilt.

I can remember feeling that my life was out of whack, the existence I was living wasn't good for me, I was on the periphery of someone else's life, just being taken along for the ride. I wasn't achieving anything, I wasn't contributing to anything. Sure, I wanted to be an author one day and write and illustrate children's books, I would tell people that I was working on something, and I was, but I couldn't take it to the next level, I couldn't be brave and show anyone what I'd done. I know now that 'procrastination' runs through me like a stick of rock *(if I manage to get this letter to you finished and posted it will be a bloody miracle)*, but back then I'd never even heard of the word. I just knew that there was an invisible brick wall a mile high in front of me, and for no good reason, I had no intention of trying to smash it down. I would just have a little scrape at the cement holding all the bricks together once in a while, then I would shelve the idea, file it away and move on to something else to almost achieve. Of course, now I understand that my behaviour boils down to fear. It's not just a fear of failing though, it's fear of losing a dream. If I haven't failed at something, then the dream that one day I might actually achieve it can stay alive.

Whilst living my shallow life abroad though, I knew that I needed to find something that would make me whole. So, I decided that what we needed most was a baby.

Just me, not him, he was quite happy with how things were, no, it was just me.

We came home, got married and almost immediately I got pregnant. I was thrilled, I was special, I was precious, and I was finally doing something important, no one could doubt that, I was growing a baby and I was having the best pregnancy that anyone had ever had in the whole world, ever.

I started nannying for some friends of friends, which I completely loved, the children adored my growing bump and were intrigued by having a pregnant person in the house. I loved the whole family and craved to have what they had as a family unit. I quickly learnt to copy how they spoke and to adopt the same style as the Mum of the family. In my mind, they were the successful happy family I wanted and was hoping I was going to get.

My new husband really wasn't that interested in me now that he had lost his drinking buddy. The fact that I was constantly banging on about sensible cars and antenatal classes didn't fire him up much either. He was hell bent on continuing to live the life we'd had abroad. Out drinking every night, Jack-the-lad, Mr Life and Soul of any party.

I felt hurt and a very real sadness that I'd got the wrong man for the job. He didn't want what I wanted and if I was really honest, I had always known that. I was scared though, if I couldn't have a life with him, what if I never met anyone else, what if nobody else wanted me, what if I had to live with just me?

On the outside, we were doing well, inside we were not. I didn't trust him, not one bit, not in any way. But I didn't say a word. I didn't know how to start the conversation and I didn't have anything solid to pin any accusations on. I knew money was tight, he was constantly reminding me of that fact, but if money was so tight how could he be dressed in designer clothes and out partying every night? It didn't add up, nothing made sense, I was scared. I wasn't in control, I had made sure that I wasn't in control and now I realised how little I actually knew about the life I was living and the man I was married to. I also realised how little I truly knew about myself.

Even though things didn't stack up financially, I had to trust him to pay the bills and keep us afloat. It was when I was asleep every night that the enormity of my fears would play out, it was always the same nightmare, I was driving my car towards a local stone bridge and all of a sudden I would lose control, no brakes and no steering, as I careered into the side of the bridge. I would always wake up screaming, sweating and shaking.

I did eventually try to talk to him, in a roundabout kind of way, but he wasn't having any of it, he thought I was being stupid and just didn't understand. I wasn't brave enough to make too much of a fuss and I already believed that I was stupid, he was the clever one, so I pushed it all down into the depths of my mind, convinced myself I was being silly and carried on living on the surface where all was lovely, and my baby bump was getting bigger by the day.

....

My beautiful daughter was finally born, and I instantly felt love for her that I couldn't ever have imagined feeling before. She became my life, my whole reason for being. I remember gazing at her asleep in her little plastic crib in the hospital and promising her with tears pouring down my cheeks that with all the power in my heart and soul I would love and protect her forever. I was going to be the best Mummy in the whole world and she would always be happy.

I believed so much in my love and duty to protect her that the sheer feeling of it all would make me feel invincible, like I could bring down an army if it threatened her. Just looking at her perfect little body nestled into mine would dissolve me with the most incredibly powerful love.

If someone had told me then, that eleven years later I would have to be separated from her because I was a danger to her I would have told them they were insane and would refuse to believe it was even possible.

But that is exactly what happened.

...

It wasn't long before my marriage was properly failing, but I didn't want to look at that, I was far too busy being the best Mummy ever.

The nightmares, however, were more powerful than ever. The resentful poison and the pure white fear that had been swilling around in me for what seemed like forever, would bubble up and let loose waking me up in the middle of the night in a pool of sweat and tears.

During the day though, I was Mary Poppins. I was soon pregnant again and had another great nine months ahead of me of being precious and special. This time though I already had a toddler.

My husband had shown very little interest in our daughter, other than to pose for photos holding her. If he was actually in during the evening, he would kiss the top of her head to say goodnight before I lumbered up the stairs with her to try and settle her down.

I would ask and ask for him to help me bath her or take her for a walk, but he simply didn't want to. Huge resentments were building up in me every day, like the bright red bricks of a new housing estate going up, one that seems to appear overnight and once it's there you can't remember the beautiful view and the open countryside that used to be in its place.

I'm a puker, if I feel sick I'm going to be sick. The morning sickness this time around was awful.

Obviously having a toddler there was no feeling sorry for myself, but apart from my Mum and friends I had absolutely no help at home from my now largely absent husband.

I'm not going to go on and on about how shit I felt and how angry and let down I was, but one evening really stands out;

We had just come home from somewhere, he had hated every minute of it and wanted to drop me and our daughter off as soon as possible so he could go straight to the pub. I had been retching all the way home and felt awful. Once we were parked in the drive I tried to get our daughter still in her car seat out of the car. I was really struggling as I was hugely pregnant by now, I was also thinking that I was literally going to throw up all over my baby. He just sat in the driver's seat watching me struggle whilst shouting at me to hurry up in-case I puked on the car.

I can't begin to tell you how angry and sad I felt, and how quickly new red bricks of resentment flew up in my mind.

Did I ask him to help me, did I call him a lazy bastard and shout at him for being horrible? No, I apologised, rushed towards the house and threw up on the door mat.

I remember listening to my daughter crying whilst I was standing in the kitchen wiping the sick off my face with a tea towel and watching the car headlights move away down the road, taking him to the local pub, to revel again in what a man he was. A toddler and a baby on the way whilst he spent the whole night trying to stare down girls tops or up their skirts.

I bloody hated him at that moment.

It was all the occasions just like that one, that not only created new resentments towards him but fuelled the frustration, disbelief and bitter disappointment I would later hurl, not at him but at myself.

There are hundreds more examples like this throughout my life, where I have been furious but frozen, unable to react. Deeply upset and let down, but with no idea how to handle it.

....

My beautiful son was born, and my little family was complete, and it was my family. As the children grew and developed, the bond between the three of us just got stronger. Their father became the outsider in his own home, and it suited him completely. His pub friends and work colleagues were his family, he loved his children, but he wasn't interested in being a part of their day to day lives. Eventually I just gave up and stopped asking him to come home in the evenings and it didn't take long to realise that a glass of wine on the sofa, on my own, after the children were in bed was actually rather lovely.

So this was our lives. My glass of wine gradually turned into two whilst he started shagging a barmaid.

I did everything with my children on my own, I was adamant that they would have a fun filled, reasonably educational and happy childhood, I took them out every day, to feed the ducks, go to baby and toddler groups, nursery, the park, anywhere. The only thing that separated me from literally being a single Mum was the band of gold getting looser and looser around my finger.

One afternoon in the park will always stay with me. It was Autumn, wet, cold and gloomy. My daughter was in one of the toddler swings and my son was asleep in the pushchair. I was pushing my daughter and we were giggling and chatting away, she must have been about two and a half at the time. A family soon joined us, the mum and dad were both playing and laughing with their children, they looked at one another in a way that I didn't even recognise, it was like they knew what the other was thinking, they played so beautifully with their children, shrieking and running around I watched them intently for ages until I realised that I was crying. I so, so wanted what they had, and I knew by the ache right in the centre of my heart, that I was never going to get it.

The marriage was over. Somehow, we carried on living our separate lives for another two years, he was all work and all play, and I was all Mummy, busy bringing up the children and amassing a mountain of bitterness. I didn't plan his exit speech on the morning that I delivered it, it just happened.

....

I was spreading Marmite on toast for one of the children whilst listening to him ranting on and on at me like incessant machine gun fire. I stood there with my back to him quietly spreading the toast as an immense rage boiled up inside me, I felt an enormous urge to lash out at him, to make him shut up and get him away from me. That was it, enough was enough. I calmly put down the Marmite knife turned and faced him and then told him that I wanted a divorce. Weirdly he was shocked and then utterly devastated, I on the other hand was not.

He moved out, and once he'd realised he was going to have to help us financially the hurt little boy disappeared, and the great big bully emerged. Email upon email, text upon text, phone call upon phone call chipped away at the last fragments of my brittle strength.

I was exhausted, strung out and completely down trodden, I didn't dare do all the things the solicitor told me to do, I was scared of the outcome, my husband had told me that if I went after his money he would simply stop working and we'd all be screwed, I was frightened, I was ridiculously weak, and I was being pulled form pillar to post. The only thing that gave me any peace was the three glasses of wine I would now drink every evening once the children were in bed.

The bullying got worse and as I felt myself start to disappear, the daily intake of wine went up and the start time came down.

I was using alcohol to fix my feelings and I had no idea how much danger I was in. I had crossed an invisible line, I had found my drug of choice and I honestly didn't realise what I was doing.

The wrangling over the divorce was horrendous, and it really took its toll on me, in the end I just stopped fighting and walked away empty handed.

I did get to keep a couple of things though; deep, deep resentments and a drink problem.

That was all a couple of years before I'd met my partner. So my single mum drinking, fuelled by bitterness was well and truly hard wired into me by the time I got to that cold dark garden swigging neat vodka from the bottle.

To me I had hundreds of excuses, thousands of reasons and a great big pot of self-pity to sit on and boy was I going to sit on it.

Three

Everything seemed to descend very quickly after that first night of secret garden drinking. My partner began to grow cold, and I understood why. He was deeply disappointed, worried and downright ashamed of me. I hated seeing him like that, it made me feel awful and I had been trying for ages not to feel anything I couldn't handle so I drank more and more.

Obviously by now I was the main topic of conversation between my friend and my partner, they were worried sick and were desperately trying to talk me into getting some help. I had started retching in the mornings now so reluctantly I decided to go and see my local doctor. I remember sitting in the waiting room with my friend, I felt like everyone around me knew why I was there and everywhere I looked there seemed to be posters and information on excessive drinking, I didn't dare look at them in case they were describing me.

The doctor was brilliant, we were given phone numbers, leaflets and lots of information. I was so ashamed to tell someone else what I'd been doing but after a few minutes It actually felt really good to talk about it. I agreed to arrange a meeting with an addiction counsellor once a week and to make another appointment with the doctor for a months' time.

The counsellor couldn't have been nicer to me, he said that the first thing he was going to help me to do was to significantly cut down on what I was drinking and learn to keep a drinking diary. He was really kind, someone who I would have respected and wanted to please. But I just couldn't be honest with him, I couldn't open up and talk about me, not the real stuff, not all the hidden away hurtful crap locked in my head. I started out not wanting to look at it, then I refused to look at it, then I shut-up- shop smiled sweetly and ether lied or changed the subject.

As for an honest drinking diary, well that was never going to happen, I couldn't even begin to look at exactly how much I drank so I sure as hell wasn't going to write it down and show another person.

It didn't take me long to be able to get the counsellor to talk about his wife or his children, basically anything except ME and MY drinking, naturally the next phase was the myriad of excuses as to why I couldn't make our weekly sessions. All utter bullshit of course, but I was brilliant at believing my own lies by now, so it was very easy to convince everyone else around me that I was telling the truth. If I let myself think too much I knew that I felt deeply ashamed, there were all these lovely people who really wanted to help me but I just couldn't let them, I didn't even know why, I just knew that I couldn't let anyone in, I couldn't let anything out and I couldn't stop drinking no matter what, not even out of guilt, shame, desperation, not even for the sake of my children. It was like I was a puppet and some sick puppet master had complete control over me.

It wasn't long before I was drinking in bottles rather than glasses every night, but I still believed that I was managing to hide it from my wider circle of friends and family. Although I was feeling like hell most of the time, I was still just about functioning by day, still in charge of my children, still working and still making important decisions, a lethal combination.

Out of the blue I was invited to a wider friend's birthday lunch. I had been trying to avoid seeing other people for ages, but she wouldn't be fobbed off so reluctantly I agreed to go, I arrived and shakily walked into her house dreading seeing other people. A group of my other friends were sitting around the kitchen table waiting for me, it didn't take me very long to realise that I wasn't at a birthday lunch at all, it was an intervention for me.

I was horrified and extremely embarrassed, my friends whom I love dearly, gently questioned me with tears in their eyes. They had no idea how far along the road I was, my closest friend and my partner had managed to contain things up until now, but my erratic behaviour had been noticed in the playground and one of the other Mums had smelt alcohol on my breath. So that was it, I was outed and I was absolutely mortified.

I admitted that I had a problem, I assured them that I was getting some help and I confessed to a fraction of what they thought was going on. However, I was becoming cold, I had been trying really hard to obliterate my feelings and I barely had a grip on my moral code anymore. I had lost myself to the extent that I found it frighteningly easy to lose the feelings of others. So once I got over the shock, I was just cross, I couldn't wait to get away and I drove home as fast as I could.

Looking back now I can see how self-obsessed I was, even though as it turned out it was with a false sense of self. It never entered my head that my friends might have found the whole episode extremely upsetting, never mind that they had all given up an afternoon to try and help me. At the time I just couldn't see it and I absolutely hated the fact that everyone knew my business. I become completely paranoid, I was convinced that the whole village was talking about me, so I tried to shut myself and my children away as much as possible, rushing them into school late to avoid the playground and taking sick days off work.

I was a full on, break neck drinker, and anyone who was capable of pricking my conscience was to be avoided. I didn't want to feel bad, I didn't want to feel anything, that was the whole point. I just wanted to get away with everything I did and everything I said, I just wanted to be left alone in the centre of my web. I never wanted to face up to anything or feel any uncomfortable twinges on the thread I had wrapped myself up in.

More than anything I wanted to be invisible and for everyone else to just go away.

One afternoon my close friend, the one who had been by my side and who is also my children's Godmother told me she was picking my children up from school to take them to her house for tea. Quite simply they didn't come back. They had told her that they were scared of how poorly I was, that they could hear me being sick every day and that they were scared of me, not because they thought I might hurt them, but because I just wasn't Mummy anymore.

That was it, the enormity of what was happening to me blew up. No one was prepared to be a bystander anymore. I was in pieces without my children, I absolutely lost the plot and went on a massive drinking binge. My partner scooped me up and took me to his house, he took my car keys off me and then got me written off work.

The pain was unbearable. The realisation that I had lost my babies, my whole reason for living, the two most precious things that I will ever have because they wanted to feel safe and as they didn't feel safe with me, that meant being away from me. I couldn't believe what I had become, I absolutely despised myself.

Having now lost all responsibility for my life I literally let go and fell. I span out of control, I didn't even try to hold on to any sanity that I might have had left, I let myself and my world crumble around me, and I drank as hard as I could around the clock not to feel it.

My mind was constantly like a washing machine on spin cycle, I believed I was possessed, I was literally bursting out of my skin and the only way I could get it all to just shut up and give me some peace was to drink to oblivion. The second the binge had worn off and I woke up the craziness would fire up again but progressively worse every time, so much more shame and guilt to shovel in, so much more remorse and failure to add, like feeding the furnace of a runaway steam train that is careering ever faster along a shortening track.

I was done in, during the following weeks I became a grotesque caricature of the person I used to be in a sick cartoon version of a life I used to live.

No one could understand why I'd become like this, no one could see why I hadn't been able to stop, why I had let this happen to me. They believed that I had a choice, pick up the bottle / don't pick up the bottle, simple. I was screamed at, shaken, pleaded with and locked in a room, but nothing could stop me. All I could do was scream back that I couldn't help it.

And when I was gently asked why, all I could whisper was that I just didn't know.

It was like every single fibre and nerve ending in my body was craving alcohol, every thought process, every breath, everything. Even when the smell of it made me retch I still had to have it.

My children were surrounded by people who loved them and I could see them now and again, but to maintain a sober-ish level long enough to sound 'normal' to them would make me start vomiting and shaking.

Very quickly they became withdrawn and pale. I could see what the situation was doing to them and it absolutely ripped my heart out.

I was lucky though, I later found out that the children's headmaster had asked my friend if she thought the school ought to get social services involved. She told him that the children were safe and happy with her and that she was working with their grandparents to protect them from being too affected by me!

Behind the scenes everyone was working together to get me into Rehab, eventually a place came up and I was told I had a couple of weeks to wait. I was relieved and absolutely desperate to go.

Everyone was counting the days down, they were all beside themselves, my partner was looking after me, he was exhausted, and I was very, very ill.

I was bloated, filthy, my hair was like felt and I had

become a really nasty person. In my slightly sober moments I was desperate for a solution. For my own safety my Mother had to sit with me every day when my partner was at work and I was utterly vile to her, I shouted, screamed and cried like a baby. The constant look of fear and pity etched on her face enraged me, she was a physical manifestation of my guilt and shame and I couldn't stand it.

I could barely keep any alcohol down. I hated what it had done to me, but ironically without enough coarsening through my bloodstream I was in danger, it had turned into my lifeline and it completely and utterly disgusted me. We had been told by the doctor that my body could go into shock and there was a chance I could start fitting if I didn't have a certain amount of alcohol inside me. I was living off Port, brought by my Mother which made her cry in the supermarket every time she was sent out to get more. I was vomiting or dry retching constantly, I wet my pants every time I retched, I missed my children so badly that I kept hallucinating that they were with me and I was so bat shit crazy I wanted to run in front of a train to stop it all. I even tried to get out of the house in the middle of the night to do just that. Luckily, I could barely walk properly so crashed down the stairs and woke my partner up who literally had to rugby tackle me back into the safety of our bedroom. I was furious with him.

He was at his wits end with me.

One image that I think I will always remember is sitting naked on the loo one morning, quietly watching my own bright red blood and mucus slowly trickle down the whole length of the white enamel bath towards the plug hole as I repeatedly retched into it, thinking that I would never be well again and I would never have my life back.

Finally the day came, and I went into treatment.

Four

I was extremely nervous as I walked into the building, I remember quietly telling a nice - looking lady my name, age, address etc. Then I said a very tearful goodbye to my partner and shuffled into a room where my bags were checked for alcohol, drugs, weapons, a phone and any form of social media device. Once everyone was happy, I was then taken to see the doctor. I can't remember much except feeling sincerely apologetic and excruciatingly embarrassed by my appearance and the very fact I was being admitted. I tried really hard to put a brave face on it and show all the kind strangers that I was an OK person, not a lying, snivelling, self-destructive nutcase which of course they could see I absolutely was. They were all really kind to me and just went about processing my arrival like ticking off a school register.

It was the run up to Christmas, there were cheerful decorations everywhere, all I could think of was my children and how far away I was from them and that I would be until the end of January. We had only been apart at Christmas a couple of times before, when they had been with their father. Now we were 250 miles apart and my only hope of sharing the next Christmas with them was to throw myself into a programme of trust, abstinence, openness and honesty, all of which I was absolutely terrified of.

I started a course of prescribed medication to wean my body carefully off alcohol and I was given pills to stop me feeling sick. Then I was shown around by one of the girls who had been in a few weeks already, she was my allotted buddy and she was lovely.

I couldn't believe how freely everyone spoke about their addictions, I was so used to hiding it and suffering at home alone, everyone was interesting and heart-breaking all at the same time. I quickly made some friends and loved being a bit of a mother hen to the younger ones, I was nearly forty and some of them were in their late teens and early twenties.

The whole basis of the recovery programme was the twelve-step programme of either AA (Alcoholics Anonymous) or NA (Narcotics Anonymous).

In my whole pitiful drinking career, it had never occurred to me to go to AA, why would I, after all, alcoholics are people sitting on a park bench drinking special brew out of a paper bag! Not a seemingly respectable mother of two young children. My ignorance could have cost me my life, it had certainly wrecked a bloody great big chunk of it.

We had a group session every morning at 10am sharp, part of the programme is to say your name and add ether alcoholic or addict or both. Even with my new-found knowledge and the years of drinking alcoholically I still fought against adding alcoholic to my name, for me it carried such a stigma, a label and a life sentence.

From my understanding nowadays, an alcoholic is someone who has an all-encompassing, uncontrollable, physical and mental reaction to the chemical ethanol, (alcohol). It doesn't matter how pretty and appealing the packaging is or how fabulous the advertising makes it look that's simply what it is, a colourless chemical that affects our brains and changes how we feel, think and behave.

From what I've heard some people say, they believe that they had been born predisposed to develop a form of the reaction the first time they took a drink, others like me, develop it over time by abusing alcohol. It doesn't matter, eventually it's the same for all alcoholics, one drop is too much and a whole ocean is just not enough.

....

Once I'd got over myself and accepted that I was a raging alcoholic, I started to really enjoy myself and my new-found temporary life. Just waking up in the early hours of my first morning in there without feeling sick and shaky was miraculous. I managed to have a shower and wash my hair, I even put some make up on and took a bit of time over my appearance.

We all had breakfast together, all washed up then split

up into our different groups and went off for our group sessions.

It was fascinating listening to everyone's lives, issues, loves and losses. We all worked together to help each other try and understand why we drank or drugged and what we could do to help us recover, I tried really hard to help people, I offered advice and got people to open up and talk about themselves. We started doing step work using the Big Blue Book of AA.

I found it all quite easy, I didn't feel the need to read the Blue book too thoroughly, I got the gist of it and could write a reasonable essay, so I was fine. I chatted to my counsellor easily, his little boy was doing brilliantly and was growing up fast. The weeks flew by, Christmas came and went, my children came to visit with my Mum and everyone couldn't believe how well I looked.

I went to a few AA meetings, I thought they were all lovely people, but too 'Goddy' for me and I didn't really pay too much attention to what they were saying. Anyway I was feeling great and it was nearly time to go home, all fixed, all sorted and ready to get my life back. One thing that always stuck in my mind though was this one girl who came in and shared my room with me and two other girls. She started talking to us one night. and I had never heard anything so awful in my whole life, the abuse and hell she had lived through was the stuff of nightmares. I wept listening to her and desperately wanted to help her. As far as I could see, she had every right to be an alcoholic/addict, anyone who'd suffered what she'd been through would be. It made me wonder what the hell I had to complain about.

Over the course of a few days, she hooked up with one of the lads even though everyone is there to recover and not to get entangled in a relationship, so relationships are extremely frowned upon. One afternoon I headed into our bedroom to find her stuffing all her clothes into a bin liner, she told me she was running off to start a new life with the lad she'd only just met a few days before. I begged her not to go, to wait and finish her stay but she just wouldn't listen. I ran down to the staff room and banged on the door, I told the counsellors what she and the lad were planning. One of them went to talk to her and the other one talked to me. She said "We can't stop them, everyone is here because they have a desire to stop drinking or drugging, if people want to leave that is up to them, only they can do the programme for themselves we cannot force sobriety on people who don't want it or, who are just not ready for it yet, maybe you should start looking after yourself and stop trying to sort everyone else out, it's not your job, it's theirs".

I didn't understand, I just got cross and yelled at her to stop having a go at me and to go and save the girl. She just smiled and walked back into the staff room.

The girl and the lad left, hand in hand with bin liners over their shoulders they just walked out of the door. I was really upset and muttered about all the complaints I was going to make. I couldn't believe that with everything the girl had been through she was turning her back on a chance to make some kind of peace with it all and find a way to live in sobriety, and I couldn't believe the counsellors just stood by and let them walk out. We were all a bit subdued after that and I still wonder what happened to them.

The next few weeks flew by, I felt great and had really enjoyed my time. I'd missed my children like crazy and couldn't wait to get home and be a family again.

There was one girl who I didn't gel with, she kept telling me in group sessions that I wasn't authentic, I told her that she didn't know what she was talking about, She had it in for me and really used to push my buttons, she would even try and wear me down if she sensed I was holding back. I just avoided her and always managed to change the subject if she directed the group at me, I mean who the hell did she think she was anyway.

Finally, it was time to go home, I had a nice neat folder full of essay's, an after-care day programme to attend and a local AA meeting near my home that I promised to go to so I was all set for my new life.

I'd had a lovely time, I loved those around me, I had learned a lot about alcoholism, about my fellow sufferers and about various therapies. I asked questions, I participated in group chats, I read out my life story to thirty people, (leaving out the really crunchy, uncomfortable bits!) I loved my six weeks in there. The biggest thing I managed to achieve however was to miss the point entirely. I didn't, wouldn't and still couldn't look at me.

Five

I had a long way to go.

Putting down the drink is a wonderful starting point but it is only the starting point. A very quick second to that has to be learning why you nearly drank yourself to death in the first place so you don't pick it straight back up again the moment something uncomfortable happens.

Learning not to pick it up again takes commitment and in most cases real desperation and a willingness to take a good look at yourself, to learn and be honest about what you find. Now I truly believed I was desperate. Any normal person would have been, but you see I hadn't been normal for a long time. Sadly, even after everything I had done and been through, I quickly realised that I just hadn't been desperate enough.

A desperate person would go to any lengths to achieve

their goal, I was a desperate drunk and I was prepared to go to any lengths to get alcohol. I would lie, cry and I would have driven to the other end of the country if it meant I would get to drink. But for sobriety I just wasn't desperate or brave enough to get stuck in to what was inside of me.

I just wanted to get fixed and go home, never drink again and push it all under the table.

I had got my counsellor to talk about himself to take the heat off me, which seemed to work so I had used that with everyone. I had done my six weeks and wasted my six weeks, but I felt great physically and I bounced out full of beans and ready to get my family back.

****

My partner knew I wasn't fixed and told me so. I told him that he was being a bloody kill joy and a cynical bastard. I had been away for six weeks; didn't he realise how awful that had been for me?

So back to being a full time Mum, my two little scruffy dogs back, all back to 'normal' and back on track.

For a while after I came out of treatment all was fine.

I took myself off to my arranged after care day programme as planned. But as I felt great, I told them that I didn't need to continue with the programme and that I was going back to work instead. The chap that ran the day programme raised an eyebrow but didn't try and talk me out of my decision so off I skipped back to the car.

I went back to work and started to face the carnage I had left behind. It was really weird to see things I had written in my daily note book. My writing didn't look like mine, it was all scrawly and didn't make sense, my filing was a mess and there were obvious mistakes in everything I'd done. It was weird, I was sober and I was looking straight at the aftermath of the drunk me.

I quickly set about sorting everything out and tried not to dwell on it all too much.

The trouble was I'd started to feel increasingly uncomfortable in my skin. You see because I had been merrily telling everyone that I was fixed, they thought it would be okay to tell me just how much I had hurt them when I'd been drinking and how glad they were that I was OK now and that I must never do that to my friends and family again. Hearing the stories over and over again of my horrendous behaviour and the pain I had caused were excruciating, but that was nothing compared to the memories that came flooding back to me of the things I'd done. The risks I'd taken, the levels of deceit I'd lived by and fact that none of it had meant anything to me at the time.

Now, that hurt. I thought I'd hated myself before, but this was a whole new ball game. I had guilt, shame, remorse and regret to deal with in spades, with no way of turning the clock back and because I'd taken such great care not to learn anything in treatment, I had no idea how to handle it. I wouldn't give AA another chance as I'd been to my local meeting and decided that it wasn't for me They were all too nice and too honest, but worst of all they could see straight through my bullshit. I quickly realised that I had shot myself in the foot, I had not listened, I had failed to register every bit of wisdom that had been so freely and kindly given to me.

I don't want you to think I'm beating myself up. I am but, I'm not. You see, it's horrible to tell you all of this, to confess everything and bare my soul because I still can't believe it was me. But it was, and it was real and I need to tell you because it reminds me of where I've come from. Not so that I can keep looking back, but so that I don't forget.

So, there I was, full of guilt and shame, still full of all the historical crap that I hadn't looked at and hanging on to being sober by a fraying thread.

****

I was aching not to drink again. As much as it hurt, I thought that really understanding just what I had done to the people I love would give me the willpower I needed to stay sober. I soaked up all my personally inflicted horror stories and encouraged people to be really brutally honest with me. However, the pain was unbearable. It was like molten lava bubbling inside me, I was desperate to numb it, desperate for it to go away, desperate to run, to stop feeling again. Willpower and guilt were the only things keeping me from drinking.

But, believe me when I say WILLPOWER and GUILT are not enough. If we could use willpower to control ourselves, there would be no need for slimming clubs, fitness books, gambling, cocaine, over eaters, alcoholics anonymous. We would all be in control and have our lives sorted. I knew that I didn't want to drink alcoholic drinks but I knew that I needed alcohol, I needed something, anything to numb myself again. I just couldn't stand being in my own skin any more so I found a vile solution - *I drank mouth wash.*

It was absolutely disgusting, it made me gag and have awful diarrhoea. But it shut my head up. I didn't want to enjoy drinking alcohol again, I wanted it to hurt and to feel as bad on my body as I knew its effect would be on my mind. I hated it and everything it stood for, but I knew it was the only thing that would stop me having feelings. Those closest to me could see me crumbling and I bloody hated that. I wanted to hide it, not face what was happening to me and prayed "Please God, don't make me go through it all again."

Six

Then it happened.

I still don't know exactly what I was thinking as I poured that first mug of wine. I suppose my soul had already left me. I was staying at my parents' house whilst they were away on holiday; my children were staying with one of my great friends' children on a sleepover. My parents had believed that I was fixed and so believed that there was no need to lock up the booze.

I quickly gulped down the mug of wine then I literally drank everything else I could lay my hands on. During the binge I can't really remember much, I just knew that I couldn't stop. It was like I'd been hijacked and someone else was driving my body. I eventually passed out on my bedroom floor.

It was the pain that woke me up, I was in agony, huge gripping waves of nausea and stomach cramps ripped through me, again and again. I was sick too many times to count, I was lying in a pool of wee and vomit and I was shaking violently, I couldn't walk, I couldn't talk. I just whimpered and tried to cope with it.

I felt so ill, that I actually believed I was going to die. I had no reason not to believe it. My heart was hammering in my chest and I had drunk enough to kill a man twice my size. That was when it hit me. For the very first time during my drinking I realised that I really didn't want to die, and I certainly didn't want to die a drunk. The terrifying thing was that right there and then, I knew that the choice had been taken out of my hands. I had no idea what damage I had done to myself and I had no idea if I was going to live or not. I was curled up on the floor, sweat pouring out of me, in complete agony and utterly terrified. The horror of the pitiful monster I had become engulfed my brain and I believed I would never get up again. There were three of us in the room that night, alcoholism, death and finally my True Self, the spirit in me that was not afraid to fight.

I finally knew that I wanted to live and I wanted to live sober. I wanted a life, a proper life. I put my hands together and I prayed and begged and pleaded for a miracle, for help, for freedom and for recovery.

I knew that night that I was beaten. Alcohol had taken me down and there was nothing in that moment that I could do about it except hope and pray that I would survive. I'd hit my rock bottom and I'd come to know desperation.

I went through hours of horrendous pain, but with each hour that passed I started to feel a little bit of hope. Slowly, through the agony I realised that I had seen the end, I was lying on the sheet of ice that had been under my feet the whole time, slowly sliding me closer and closer to an alcoholic death. Below the ice was my grave but above me was a life. Alcohol was bigger than me, infinitely more powerful and if I drank again it would smash the ice I was lying on and drop me into my grave in a heartbeat. The only thing to do was to trust that I had found the answer and stick to it, no matter what. I knew that I must remember the pain that I had just been through, that I had been lucky, that the only way I had any chance of stopping my own early death was to hang onto my new found discovery that I must NEVER, EVER pick up an alcoholic drink again and I must immerse myself in recovery.

....

Finally coming to believe that I was truly powerless over alcohol literally saved my life. My drinking nearly took everything away from me, physically yes, that was obvious, but the real damage was in my head and my heart. I could not believe it had happened to me. Alcohol had made me become a monster and yet sickeningly I knew that if I ever drank again I would just want more.

Only when I surrendered and knew that I was beaten, that alcohol had won, did I find my path to freedom.

The next few days were horrendous, my partner picked me up and took me back to my house. He told me that he couldn't cope with me anymore and was ending our relationship. My dear friend who had my children told me that they did not want to come home and they didn't trust me anymore. My friend who had been with me every step of the way turned up at my house and absolutely let rip at me, she screamed and shouted and completely annihilated me, the only thing I could scream back at her was that I was a monster.

My mum came back from holiday and rushed to my side. She was amazing, we both sobbed for ages and then we made a plan. She took me to see my Boss, I was incredibly nervous and expected to lose my job. I explained everything to him and he immediately wrote me off work for another month - he couldn't have been more supportive. I phoned the day programme and got myself booked in to start the next day, then I found an AA meeting nearby and just turned up. I cried the whole way through the meeting, relief and shock hitting me in equal measures. The biggest thing that hit me though was the realisation that throughout the last 24 hours I had not once craved alcohol. A switch had flicked off inside me and all I had to do now was learn not to switch it back on again.

Sitting and sobbing in that AA meeting felt like coming home, the people were just so kind, they all understood how I felt and not one of them judged me. I quickly learnt that it was a spiritual programme not a religious one, the word God meant a higher power of your own understanding, whether that was the God found in church or in the power of an ancient tree, it didn't matter, it literally could be anything. Everyone there were all just people like me, but they had found a solution to living a life free of alcohol and to the absolute fullest. They believed that recovery is all about progression not perfection. They were happy and funny, and they gave me hope.

I met up with one of the ladies after the meeting and she explained how it all worked to me. She said that AA was referred to as 'The Rooms', that the only requirement to be a part of AA is a desire to stop drinking and to live a life free of alcohol. There were no fees, just a donation that you could afford to give at the end of every meeting. She explained that as soon as possible I needed to find myself a sponsor, this would need to be someone that I had heard talk in meetings, that

I felt a connection to, and someone with a good deal of sobriety under their belt. They would then take me through the steps outlined in the Big Blue Book and be there for me every single day, either on the end of the phone or in person. The most important thing she told me, was that AA was based on anonymity. 'The Rooms' were a safe place where you could talk openly about yourself without fear of being gossiped about, this was the only thing that was asked of everyone who walked through the door, it is the very foundation of safety and shelter that AA offers. She added that there was no such thing as an unproductive meeting, there were always lessons to be learnt and identifications to find. All I had to do was look for the similarities not the differences, open my ears and listen.

I walked into the day programme the following day a different person. The chap I had seen before, asked me why I was back. I told him, "I thought I was fixed, but I was wrong, I didn't need to get fixed, what I needed was to pull myself apart".

He just raised an eyebrow, introduced himself as my

tutor and told me to sit down, he then started talking to the class about the power of ego!

The day programme was based on the twelve steps of AA, our tutor taught us the principals of how to start going through the steps, we were expected to go to AA meetings in the evenings and immerse ourselves in the programme. Our tutor was a hard-talking Scottish man, with eyes that could look into your soul, there was absolutely nothing he hadn't seen, done, tried or got someone else to do. He was the most difficult person I have ever met in my entire life, he made my blood boil, he made me cry with frustration, he challenged everything I said and everything I thought. But he cemented a recovery programme into me that changed my outlook on life entirely.

I wrote and read and pulled every part of myself and my behaviour apart. In a few short weeks I had learned the basis of living life on life's terms. I understood that the solution for me lay in what I was prepared to learn about myself and then how I was going to either cherish what I found or let go of it.

I learnt that there were many layers to a healthy mind, I started to learn how to meditate and how to try and be mindful. I learnt about the power of my breath and how to try and ground myself, I found that I loved walking and yoga and I learnt that there is always hope if we just trust in something that is infinitely bigger than us, our very own higher power.

....

I discovered my part in the breakdown of my marriage, and my part in all the other unhealthy relationships I have had, including food, shopping and my desire to self-sabotage. I was shown that by working the twelve steps I could finally find acceptance and peace with my past and a healthy framework to base my future on.

Most of all I learnt that I was forever going to be a work in progress, to maintain my sparkly new life as a sober person, I would have to be vigilant of my wayward mind, always gently checking that I wasn't quietly building another big red 'fuck it button' to press if things got unbearable again.

....

My children finally came home, it was a complete epiphany for all three of us. I was really nervous as they walked back into our house, they were still holding hands with my friend, they looked so little and so scared. I quietly knelt down and held out my arms, fat silent tears trickled down my face.

My daughter stood in front of me and locked her huge eyes onto mine, she studied me for what seemed like ages "You look different" she said in a small crackly voice, then she let go of my friend's hand and flung herself at me. My son immediately followed suit. We clung onto each other laughing and crying as my friend quietly left us. I will never forget burying my face in their necks and mentally thanking a universe of lucky stars that my prayers had been answered, I had my children back and I was never, ever going to lose them again. As the day's ticked by I finally learnt to accept that I'd lost my partner and my best friend, they just couldn't give me another chance. Nobody trusted me not to drink again, which was fine because I trusted me. I knew that I was finally in recovery, and I was prepared to learn how to live with the fall out of my past.

....

That was all six years ago now and although my life is by no means perfect, it's heading in a good direction. My partner and I tried incredibly hard to make our relationship work again, but there was just too much damage done to save it. I will always love him, and I will always be grateful to him for having the guts to be the first person to pull me up on my drinking and stand by me for as long as he did.

My children are thriving and as a family we are stronger than ever. They are both looking forward to going to university over the next couple of years. My daughter finds the issue of addiction fascinating and something she's thinking about studying in the future. When my son isn't eating me out of house and home, he's studying maths and biology. Most importantly they seem to be pretty happy, well balanced and really funny people. I am lucky enough to have my friend back, what happened to us changed everything for ages, but we are now back to how we were before I ever picked up a drink, basically a couple of complete idiots who find the same stupid things hilarious. I read my Big Blue Book from cover to cover many times over and I continue to work at the twelve steps. It's a daily programme, all I have to do is use what I have learned to stay sober for 24 small hours at a time. I have met the most incredible people along the way and have witnessed the terribly sad demise of a few that just didn't get it in time. So, my run up, leap and crashing fall are really not that special, I don't have a good enough reason for destroying my children, my family and my friends. I can't give you one real justified excuse for why I picked my life up with two hands and drank it, and I certainly don't have anyone else to blame. I have met people who have lost their children, wife, husband, home etc. but they have not thrown themselves into a bottle and I have met people who break a nail and it's enough to make them reach for a drink. I suppose how we deal with our own personal suffering is all relative to us, there is nothing to gain from comparing our lives in terms of success, failure or levels of pain to another person.

In my recovery I have met hundreds of people who, in my perception, suffered so much more than me, fell so much harder than me and relapsed so many more times than I did. But all of that doesn't matter a jot in a room filled with years of sobriety and recovery.

I can recognise myself in every single problem drinker that I meet, whether that's in 'The Rooms' in a meditation class, or out walking my dogs. I don't feel the need to tell anyone outside The Rooms that I am an alcoholic, and I know that nobody in The Rooms will be discussing me either. I feel free to get on with my life without a label or a stigma attached to me.

I often get asked why I don't drink and I simply say that a few years ago I nearly drank myself to death, so I just don't do it anymore. I am more than happy to talk honestly about my journey if they want to know more, but most people are just happy with my answer and we carry on chatting about something else. I wanted to write this letter to you so that you could look for any similarities between us, within your own life.

I wanted to let you know that if you do identify with anything I've said you are not alone, there is strength to be found in unity and there is freedom to be had in understanding. Every day I continue to learn that I'm not special or different, I'm incredibly lucky to be just like millions of people of all backgrounds all around the world. I am truly grateful to be well and sober enough to write this letter to you, and I am truly blessed to know that if I ever I feel like I will fall again, all I have to do is reach out and I will be carried.

Take care, know that I'm thinking of you and take my love, always. xxx

PART TWO
Living on Dry Land

Hi, how are you doing?

I hope you found a few minuets to read my last letter and more than anything I hope it didn't make you pull down the shutters or worse still, think "Well I'm not as bad as her so therefore I don't have a problem".

Remember, I wasn't that bad in the beginning ether, as I have said, alcoholism is progressive. It catches up with you. Thankfully my drinking career was short, but if I had remained in denial for much longer than I did, I simply wouldn't be here now, I wouldn't have made it.

A sober life is brilliant, if you think about it, why wouldn't it be? Generally, you can get through everyday pretty much unscathed. Physically you feel great, you lose the bloatedness, your skin, eyes, teeth and hair get brighter, you have the ability to earn money and you can actually eat rather than just drink. Above all of that though is an amazing opportunity to start again, wipe the slate clean, chuck out all the rubbish in your head, remember where you have come from and move on.

You have a chance, you have a future, and all you have to do to keep it is learn how to live life on life's terms, warts an all! It's been six years since I last had a drink, **SIX** years! I can't believe it. I couldn't even imagine lasting six minutes during the height of my drinking. So how have I done it, how have I gone from a lost cause to a reasonably normal, reasonably capable and extremely grateful individual?

You may be wondering why I'm not banging on about my new found glamorous, wealthy life, littered with worthy anecdotes and tales of wondrous achievements. How have I come through so much and yet the best I can hope for is to be reasonably normal?

Quite simply, getting sober and living in recovery gives you back the life you stopped living when your addiction replaced your free will. Sobriety doesn't turn you into a Super hero, you don't receive a ready made whole new life the minute you put down the drink and choose recovery. If you want a new life, you have to be prepared to carve it out for yourself. You may not get a super hero cape and pants for surviving alcoholism, but you do get a future, and for me that's more than enough. Considering myself as 'normal' is bloody amazing and a complete miracle. When I was in the early stages of recovery my goal was to get my life back, nothing else was more important to me, my sole aim was to be a good mum to my children, bring in a wage and pay my bills. That was it, I knew how much I had lost and I was finally prepared to go to any lengths to get it back. There's no big magical secret, I just gave in and admitted to myself that I was an alcoholic. I was finally prepared to listen and I stopped looking for an argument as to why I wasn't a problem drinker, alcohol abuser or a drunk and honestly accepted the fact that I was all of the above and worse. I didn't want to be that person anymore, I didn't want to knock red wine over people's suits in the pub, or throw up in people's beautifully maintained front gardens on the way home, or hide empties all over my house and garden.

I even hid bottles in my daughter's wardrobe, I remember thinking, well she never puts anything away, so she'll never see them. Of course, she did, she was 11yrs old, she was rummaging around looking for some shoes and found piles of bottles under all her old toys and teddys. I can remember her little face as she quizzed me, a mixture of terror, confusion and anger swimming in her huge worried eyes.

I will never say my past sits well with me, it absolutely doesn't. The full shock of what became normal everyday behaviour still haunts me now, but rather than letting the enormous guilt and shame of it all drag me down, I turn it around. You are going to think I'm mad, but I'm grateful for the scars I have both mental and physical from my active drinking days, because they form a part of the many rock solid reasons why I don't go back, back to the insanity that is always only the length of my forearm away from me.

I would so love for you to have read my last letter and for it to have worked like a magic spell, releasing you from any insatiable cravings you might have and saving you from the utter hell that I encountered, I wouldn't wish what happened to me on anyone. The truth is, sadly, I can't save you, no one else can, the cut throat and down-right ugly, senseless battle between any one of us who unwittingly 'crosses the line' and alcohol is one that you absolutely need to win, no matter what, and to do it, you must start from within YOU! It really is the ultimate inside job. However, as I've said you certainly do not need to do it alone.

A very good AA friend of mine once said to me, *"Never go deeply into your own mind unaccompanied"*.

The best gift I can give you, is a little bit of advice, always remember that you are worth fighting for and please try and stop lying to yourself. The quicker you can get honest, the quicker you will start to heal. I don't mean all the lies you palm off to everyone else, I mean stop lying to you. Look hard into the mirror, I know it's really difficult when you hate the reflection staring back, but keep looking, that twisted reflection soaked in all the historic fear that you can't bear to look at, will slowly fade away, and when it does you will see where to find the humility and bravery that is within you to seek some help and face your demons.

When you are ready to receive help, be very careful not

to sit in judgment, try not to look for the differences in the people you meet, instead look for the bits you identify with, believe me they are there, and they are usually in the people that you would never have chosen to chat to in your life, let alone share a deep and powerful connection with.

The people that are winning their own battles and are walking free of the white knuckle worry of where their next drink will come from, are truly special, kind and equal souls. A lot of them will really annoy the hell out of you, but just remember, that annoyance comes from within you, it's your reaction to them that you need to look at, it's not your job to point out someone else's flaws.

Go online, find an AA meeting near you, just walk through the door, sit down and listen. It's that simple. AA is the best starting point for most, and usually, it is the one that everyone comes back to.

The affect alcohol has on me and so many like me, is baffling. I honestly don't know what happens, what turns me into a devious, dangerous, utterly self-centred, completely self-obsessed and self-sabotaging force of nature.

Living for the day, each day, in sobriety I am employable, kind-ish, considerate-ish and usually quite a good laugh. Most importantly I am dependable, reliable and a reasonably useful person to have around. Just like everyone else.

That is in sobriety and sobriety is a very different thing to just not drinking.

By simply not drinking, alcoholics like me can be all of the above, sometimes for years, but more often than not, we are also 'oh so sorry, so unbelievably sorry, so convinced we will never do it again, prepared to say and do anything to prove we won't do it again. Anything that is, except being able to walk away from our next drink.

The saddest part is that we are just as shocked, horrified and destroyed as those we have hurt once again, when the shit hits the fan for the second, third and hundredth time. You see, before my relapse, I was simply 'not drinking'. I wasn't doing anything else, I wasn't looking into WHY I nearly drank myself to death in the first place.

What I'm trying to say in my usual rambling way is that there is always some kind of trigger for why we use alcohol like we do, until we can identify that trigger and disarm it, it will always be poised and ready to be squeezed once again. OK, I say this now, but remember for a very long time I didn't know about this kind of stuff.

It turned out that I'd been holding my trigger all my life and before I knew what I was doing, I had squeezed it. My weapon of choice happened to be alcohol, but it could have been food, drugs or gambling, anything to change the way I felt.

I went from someone who on occasion, overdid it and behaved in a way I would regret, to watching the clock, planning when I could drink so it looked normal and lying. Telling convincing, compelling, completely believable and brutal lies. I say brutal, because what those lies allowed me to do was to start to disassemble my and my children's lives, like breaking up a jigsaw puzzle by slowly removing the pieces one at a time, piece by piece, lie by lie.

You see, if I could just keep going, keep the level of alcohol in my blood stream at a constant feed, all day and all night, numb and painless in my cocoon, I could manage. I could look after all the important things in my life; my children, my dogs, my job, my life. But I wasn't looking after them, I was putting them in real danger, every minute of every day, without fail and what's more, if I'm honest, until I got really ill I didn't want to stop. Not really, not deep down. I just wanted to stay numb and keep on clinging on, not admitting to anyone, let alone myself, that I was disappearing.

It was the final relentless bloody beating that alcohol gave me that night at my parents' house that saved my life. I gave in, I accepted that I had lost, I was no different, I was going to be just another one of the millions of people around the globe who tragically die from an alcohol addiction.

I had **FINALLY** surrendered.

Giving in to the power of alcohol was the biggest gift

I will ever give to myself, because in that moment I prayed for my life and raised my little white flag, I finally threw the towel in and stopped the fight.

You can only fight something if you keep getting up and standing in front of it, for me that night, I simply stayed down. Nowadays there is no fight, I hold the power, and that power purely lies in my complete understanding and acceptance.

I cannot drink, and if I do It will kill me, it's that simple.

I hope you don't hit your own rock-bottom, I truly hope in my ever wishful way that you will get help and get well before you free-fall, but if you don't, I hope that you are lucky, I hope that your crash to the bottom will be catastrophically huge, involving other people, exposing you and utterly terrifying you. I don't say that lightly, I say that from the bottom of my heart because I know, that if you don't manage to stop yourself before you fall, the harder your fall is, the more likely you are to learn from it and be able to claim your freedom over your addiction. For some, their journey to rock bottom has many layers, each one that they crash through they think will be the last, until the next time when they crash again, but a lot harder this time and so it goes on until they are sharing the floor of their rock bottom with two choices; drink and die or surrender and live.

****

For some people alcohol is a pleasant distraction from everyday life, just a colourless liquid that is prettied up and disguised in a million ways to taste delicious and look appealing, fun and even harmless.

It ignites a warm glow in bodies, it helps a party go with a bang, it loosens lips and replaces shyness with confidence. But it isn't for me anymore, it's for other people, great friends of mine that can have a really boozy night, wake up with a headache, sort themselves out and get on with their day.

Of course, I used to be like that, but not now. Now my body, brain whatever the hell happens doesn't want a few drinks over an evening with friends, it wants an ocean, oblivion and people to take hostage along the way, and then it just wants more, and more.

I thought I'd never say this, but do you know what, just understanding how apocalyptic the effect of one drink will be on me, sits perfectly well with me. There's no guessing game, no 'I think I'll be OK this time', it literally is black and white. Which is fine, because thanks to the Twelve-step programme of AA, there is absolutely no reason on this earth why I'll ever need to pick up a drink again anyway.

Life with all its little surprises, still happens, people fall in and out of love, win and lose money, deals fall through, relationships flounder, people die. Sobriety doesn't put you in a little fluffy cloud where tricky or traumatic things don't happen to you, it actually puts you on to a solid and stable rock, where you can pretty much handle all the crunchy things that are thrown at you and still put a sober head on your pillow every night. It amazes me that in the last couple of years I can be the strong one in my family, I can sort the crap out and stand up when others can't. It wasn't long ago that I couldn't even brush my own hair.

My life depends on me protecting my sobriety and that must always come first. Without my sobriety I have absolutely nothing. It's like putting the oxygen mask on yourself first in an emergency so that you can help everyone else. If I'm sober my whole life then everyone associated with it is OK.

I'm sitting in the driving seat now, it's bloody hard work, I'm a single Mum and I work every day of the week. I may be attached to a strong rock but I'm still only a squishy human, so for a lot of the time I do feel completely overwhelmed by just how much I have to do and think about, and sometimes I do just want to run away, switch off the alarm clock, shut the door on it all and hide under my duvet, but I never do, not now, I get on and deal with it and soon enough I'm firing on all cylinders again.

If I do feel lonely and scared, I go to a meeting, within seconds of walking through the door I've been hugged and enquired after, I'll have a coffee in my hand and I'm usually laughing at something. Then we will all listen to a 'share' (a talk) from a recovering alcoholic on their experience, strength and hope and I will easily find one or a million things that I identify with. I will learn something, I will feel something, I will be reminded that I am no different from everyone else in the room and therefore If I need some support all I have to do is ask.

I also have my sponsor, so if for any reason I'm feeling off beam, I call her and she talks me through it, sometimes we chat for a minute sometimes it's for an hour, it doesn't matter, nothing is left to fester and cause me mental pain or heartache.

Sometimes though I do have to concede and just accept that I have to sit with stuff that can't be resolved. I can only change me, I can't change other people, including the way that they think, feel and act. I try and keep my life in some sort of perspective, I try really hard to deal with what is actually happening rather than what I think is happening. I have to be very careful not to do other people's thinking for them, what I mean by that is me making decisions on what I think another person would say, do or want. Simple example, I wear something a bit daring and then I decide what other people will think of me, so then I lose my bravery and get changed. The simple truth is that most people don't notice what I'm wearing, certainly don't give a stuff anyway and are far too busy worrying about themselves to give my dodgy outfit a second thought. (Unless of course it's my daughter who can't help but comment on my wardrobe!) So why don't I just wear what I want to and get on with my day.

Or I say or do something really stupid (actually quite a regular occurrence) and I decide that everyone around me thinks I'm an idiot, so therefore I must be. Oh and I'm probably useless, under-qualified for my job and a complete twit. Again, no one's probably even noticed that I fell over the step coming into the building or that I asked the head of my organisation how old he is, instead of just how are you? It doesn't matter, it doesn't make me a bad or useless person and whilst I'm wasting precious brain cells dwelling on my idiocy all day, no body else is giving it a second thought!

We should all just stop worrying about what other people think, if you are behaving as a decent person it really doesn't matter what other people think of you. Wear what you want, cut your hair how you want, snog who you want (as long as they are single and willing!) if you have a nice complement to give to someone, give it. We certainly don't struggle to share the bad stuff, so get on and share the good stuff. Say "Do you know what, I bloody love you!" to the people you love. If you feel like utter crap, go and do something helpful or kind for someone else. It will definitely help them, and it will make you feel a million times better than any drink or drug ever could.

***

Obviously, I am not a saint all the time, I do get cross and shouty, especially at pants left on the floor! But If I'm upset or unhappy, I have learned that I can only work on **MY** feelings, other people's behaviour is not my responsibility. It's simple, and it's one of the first things I learned from AA, I need to accept the things I cannot change (other people) and change the things I can (Me).

However, if I think I've upset someone, I absolutely have to address that as soon as possible. So, I ask them and if I have upset them, we talk about it and sort it out.

If someone has upset me, I find that much harder to deal with, so, I speak to my sponsor, I talk to my friends and I find a way to appropriately deal with the situation.

I know that sweeping resentments and fears under the carpet will only make them more powerful, so I try not to hold on to resentments and I try to face my fears, I talk to people and get stuff out, I have learned that holding on to tonnes of toxic waste in my head will serve me no purpose, so I ether need to deal with it or just let it go without any fuss.

Deep-rooted resentments are really tricky, nasty little gremlins though. I have a huge amount to work through, mainly to do with myself, my father, my ex-husband and a few other people. I will be working on those for a few more years yet, but they certainly don't affect me on a daily basis anymore.

I do a little exercise every morning when I wake up and every night before I go to sleep. I mentally tick off all the things I can think of that I am grateful for. Big or small it doesn't matter, sometimes I've had a rubbish day and I'm still sulking, so all I can tick off is that I'm grateful to have been sober for another 12 hours, at the very least that always makes me feel better, it doesn't change what's in my bank account, but it certainly changes what's in my head.

Walking the dogs and having a good old shout at the sky or into the wind really helps too.

My other saving grace is my higher power 'Rachel'. You may remember I talked about finding your own higher power in my earlier letter to you.

My understanding of a higher power, or a 'Power Greater Than Ourselves', is having something to turn to that isn't us, it can be an intense power that you have found coming from within you, but it isn't actually you. It's not your mental decision-making that's driving it. It is something that is always with you, something you can gain comfort from, something to visualise, talk to or hold. It doesn't matter what it is as long as it works for you. For some it is their Religion, or their understanding of their God, for others it is simply a special tree or a plant. For me, I found Rachel.

The whole higher power thing drove me mad, I knew that I desperately wanted one, but I just couldn't find one. Now I'm quite a spiritual type, I can easily see the beauty in a tiny dew encrusted spider web or feel the power emanating from an ancient stone building, so I thought, higher power, easy, it's just a matter of choosing what to have; The Moon, The Sun, Mother Nature. Any of those would be fine. But you have to feel it and I just didn't. I even told my sponsor that I was going to be my higher power, I had got myself into this mess and I was going to get myself out of it.

Her reply was;

"There are few things I know in life, but you do have your very own higher Power, and I can absolutely assure you, it ain't you!"
Then as ever she hugged me and giggled!
I would bring my frustration at not finding one up at

AA meetings, the old timers, the ones who had been around the rooms for many years would smile at me and assure me that I would just know, when I had found what I was looking for, it would become crystal clear. Really bloody unhelpful, which I told them, again, more laughing. But actually, if I really stopped and thought about it, I didn't really know what I was looking for.

Then one day I was out shopping, and I just thought I'd quickly pop into our local cathedral. I love churches and cathedrals, I just love the cool serenity hanging in the air, and the cloak of calm and peace that seems to wrap around you as soon as you walk over the threshold. I'm not massively religious and I'm not, not religious. But being within those walls, steeped in eons of history, soaked with millions of prayers of gratitude, guidance and desperation, I always feel humble and small. I walked about for a bit, smiled at a group of small school children who were all having a lovely time messing about whilst they were supposed to be learning about the cathedral's long history.

I sat down in one of the pews for a few minuets and just gave myself some time to think, it didn't take long before I became aware my parking ticket was about to expire, so I started getting ready to leave, but then I felt a small urge to walk further up the cathedral, so I did, and then for no particular reason I just walked into a side room. On the wall right in front of me was an inscription to woman called Rachel. I immediately locked onto it and started reading. She had died three hundred and fifty years ago on my birthday, she was only young, she had all that life ahead of her but on the date of my birthday, three hundred and fifty years before me she died. Just standing there and letting it all sink in made me cry. I was young, I had so nearly lost my life, but I had been given another chance, I was one of the lucky ones, so I resolved that for myself and for Rachel before me I was going to make sure that I didn't waste my second chance, I was going to nail this thing called recovery and I was going to take my new found higher power with me.

I did get a parking ticket though!

So, from that day on, I talk to Rachel. When I just don't know what to do, I turn it over to her, I literally hold out my hands and say, "I don't know what to do, here you go Rachel this one's for you". and I let it go and trust that somehow, eventually I will be shown the way. Amazingly it works, don't get me wrong, I don't expect Rachel to sort my entire life out for me, I don't sit around doing nothing whilst waiting for a sign. I trust and believe that nothing happens to me by chance, even the really harrowing stuff. So I know that by taking some time and waiting I will eventually know in my heart how to handle something and whatever I do it will be the right thing.

I used to react to upsetting incidents immediately, not by biting back, for me, the knee jerk reaction would ether be a flood of intense *fear*; hide, isolate, drink to numb it or *flight*; get as far away from the problem as possible, drink to numb it. By turning my troubles over to my Higher Power, I am literally freed from fear and worry, and as I said, I will then find the strength and clarity to sort all my rubbish out the best way I can at that time. Having a little bit of faith in something that isn't you, really does go a long way. I keep my eyes, ears and heart open. I try to be a decent person to have around. I keep my metaphoric front door step swept. If there are things that need to be addressed and sorted I do it. My behaviour has to sit well with me and if it doesn't, I have to change it. Other people's front door steps are not my concern. I can only work on me.

****

The dust didn't settle for a very long time after my ultimate fall to rock bottom, to be honest I know there are still particles from the fallout flying around now, but it's OK, I understand, I know that none of my friends or family will ever forget what happened to me and what watching from the sidelines did to them.

I try to be kind to myself, the guilt and shame associated with my drinking rears up now and again, but it's my inability to forgive myself that causes me pain, no one else ever puts it on to me. I have learned that to put a sober head on my pillow every night, I must look after my mental health, my physical health and how I treat other people.

The risk of a relapse is always possible. I have been told in AA that complacency, forgetting to be grateful for sobriety and believing that you are recovered are the biggest threats to a happy sober life.

And, sadly it really can happen again, I have met a few people in the rooms who have picked up a drink again after many years of sobriety, it's not that they have spent their sober years white knuckling it every day, desperately trying not to drink. No, alcohol addiction is far, far more insidious than that.

After a few years of good solid sobriety, some people can start to believe that they are recovered. They may feel strong, happy, content and healthy. They stop going to meetings, they stop keeping their doorsteps swept and they stop being grateful. Other people around them might see how well they are and start to say things like "*Surely it would be OK to have a small beer now and again, or a glass of wine with dinner, go on, you'll be fine.*" But you see it isn't fine, after six years I am still living in recovery, I feel better now than I ever have, but I am not recovered. If I was recovered, I could drink normally again, but I know that I can't drink normally again, because I don't think about alcohol normally anymore, my mind and body doesn't want just one glass of wine, it wants gallons of it. I know that today as clearly as I knew it the day after my relapse, and I'm bloody glad I do because it keeps me safe.

****

I met a lovely man in the rooms a couple of years ago, he had picked up a glass of beer again after TWELVE years of sobriety. He admitted that he had become complacent, he had stopped recognising how grateful he was for just being sober and having his life back, but most importantly, he had stopped working at the principals of the twelve steps because he had started to believe he was recovered.

His one beer turned into an enormous binge that lasted for a week. When I met him, he had been sober again for a couple of days. I will never forget the shock, remorse and mental torture etched on his face. He just couldn't believe what had happened to him after twelve amazing years in sobriety. He cried all the way through the meeting and was enveloped in love and support by every single person in the room.

Two days later very sadly he killed himself.

My local AA community was distraught, AA is a 'Fellowship of Men and Women', and it really is. People care about other people. Every suffering alcoholic that comes into the rooms, immediately becomes cared for. To lose someone like that was beyond belief and unbelievably sad. It was shocking and brutal and a chillingly stark reminder that it could happen to any one of us. There is a lot of research out there on whether an alcoholic can recover and therefore drink normally again. Personally, I don't get swept up in that, I know how I feel, and I know that I am not recovered.

Once I crossed the line and became addicted to alcohol a change happened in me that I know, for me, is irreversible. I know, because due to one of my jobs I am around alcohol a lot, and when I watch people drinking and there are bottles and bottles of wine and spirits around me, I am reminded that I don't want one or two drinks, I want all of it and I will not stop. Just knowing that makes me smile, because it reminds me that I am free. If I ever believed that I could stop after just one or two drinks then I would be in very big trouble.

I don't get everything right all the time, but as long as I'm trying, as long as I'm keeping my wayward mind in check and watching my behaviour then I can live with me. Every day I try and do the things that I know are good for me. I do my mental gratitude list, I make sure I'm up early, my children are organised, the bills are (nearly) paid. I write everything that I need to do into my diary, I write myself reminders, keep on top of the hoovering and the washing basket. I even eat the odd bloody apple!

I make sure that I fill my lungs up with fresh air. It is very important to me to get outside and blow the cobwebs away, whether its walking on a freezing cold beach in the middle of winter, riding my bike or chasing my dogs around a country park. It doesn't matter, just doing something outside makes me feel good. I love my life, and more than that, I know how extremely blessed I am to have it, to have purpose and fulfillment, to truly be a functioning member of the human race again. That morning watching my own blood and bile trickle down the whole length of that white enamel bath, I thought I'd never get my life back, but I did, I really did and so can you……….. just for today!

Take care, know that I am always thinking of you and take my love, always. xxx

About the Author

I met the author of this book a couple of years after she had surrendered in her fight with her demon - *the dreaded drink*. At that time, I would never have known she was an alcoholic, she seemed so normal. She was funny, friendly, quick witted, sociable and intelligent. She was a good caring mother and as far as I could tell, a responsible adult. But what was I expecting, had I simply not noticed her great big horns and dragon-like tail?

It was several years later that she shared her past experience with me. I was completely shocked and deeply saddened. I couldn't believe that this person I saw as such a strong, independent, capable woman had previously been such a wreck. Thinking on, I realised that she must have always been this strong, how else could she have coped with what life had thrown at her, come out the other side and still be smiling.

I know that she will never be *'recovered'* but I'm certain that alcohol hasn't beaten her and that she has learned how to cope and how to live happily, with strength and courage not from a bottle, one day at a time.

A. Friend.

38574836R00068

Printed in Poland
by Amazon Fulfillment
Poland Sp. z o.o., Wrocław